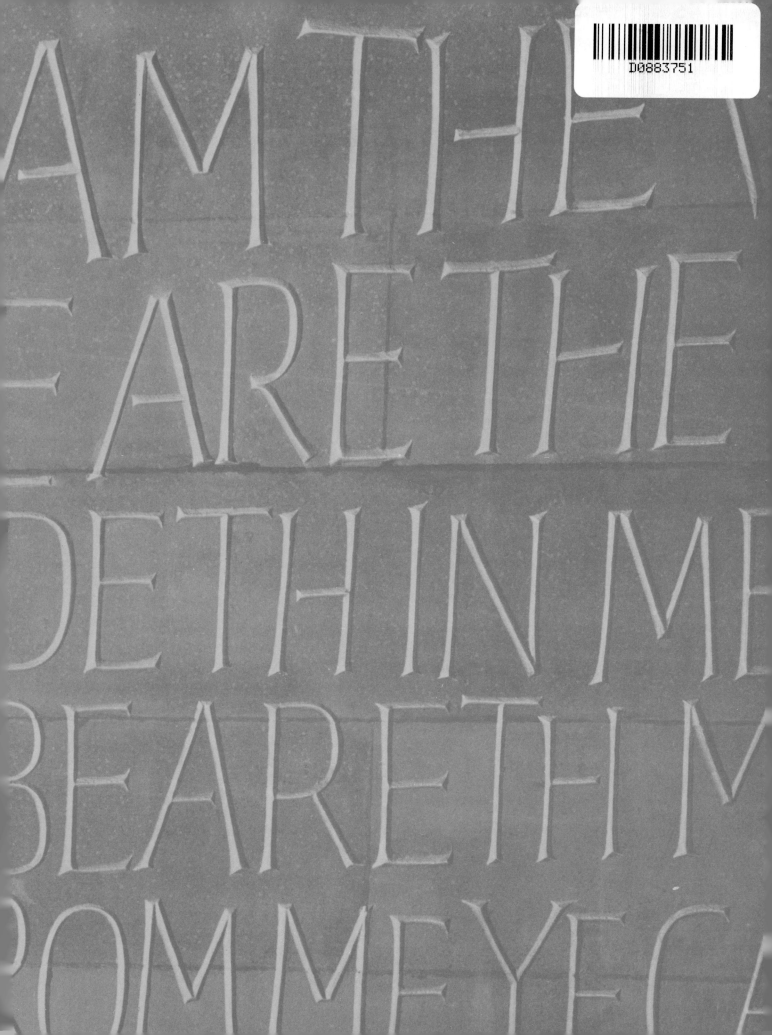

a guide to Coventry Cathedral and its Ministry

Painting of the scene of the Consecration of the Cathedral 25th May, 1962 by Terance Cuneo presented by John Laing Ltd to Coventry Cathedral

COVENTRY

a guide to Coventry Cathedral and its Ministry

CATHEDRAL

H C N Williams Provost of Coventry

photography by Richard Sadler AIBP FRSA

HODDER AND STOUGHTON LIMITED SAINT PAUL'S HOUSE WARWICK LANE LONDON EC4

BOOK DESIGNED BY COLIN BANKS AND JOHN MILES
for Hodder and Stoughton Limited

Printed in Great Britain for Hodder and Stoughton Limited
St Paul's House, Warwick Lane, London E C 4
by C Tinling and Company Limited, Liverpool, London and Prescot

contents

Due acknowledgment must be made to the help given by
the following, in enabling me to copy photographs, paintings
and drawings in the following collections:
The Herbert Art Gallery and Museum
The City Archivist
The Coventry City Libraries (Coventry and Warwickshire Collection)
All the Chairmen of the Committees controlling the above.

Also the Directors of Powell Engineering
                    W H Jones and Sons Limited
                    Courtaulds Limited
                    Sir W G Armstrong Whitworth Aircraft Limited
for permission to reproduce photographs which were their copyright.

Mention must also be made of Mr and Mrs Woodfield, who supplied the
plan showing the remains and reconstructed details
of the former Benedictine Priory and its relation to the present
Coventry Cathedral.

preface

This book sets out to do three things. First, to establish the long tradition upon which the city of Coventry and all its creative enterprise rests by sketching briefly its history. Secondly, to describe in some detail the new Cathedral as a place of architectural and artistic beauty. And thirdly – perhaps most important of all – to indicate the purpose for which the building was erected and adorned, namely, to try to declare the Christian faith to the twentieth century with renewed relevance. No one part of these intentions would be complete without the other.

Grateful acknowledgement is made to Mr F. Bliss Burbidge for permission to quote from his admirable book, 'Old Coventry and Lady Godiva' – certainly the most scholarly book available on the history of Coventry.

Statue of St Michael Overcoming the Devil by Sir Jacob Epstein

The Godiva pageant enacted in the eighteenth century;
oil painting by David Gee 1793–1871, in the
Herbert Art Gallery

The Ancient History of Coventry

Little is known about the origin of the name 'Coventry', though the two most likely explanations are that it was a well-known tree associated with the village of an important person who might have been called *Cofa*, and therefore would have given his name to the meeting place in some such form as *Cofantreo*. Or, alternatively, it could well have been a reference to the valley in which the early settlement was established, *Cofa* being an early English word for a valley or a recess, surviving in the word 'cove' today. 'Tree' would either have meant a forest or a wood or possibly a cross by the wayside, or it could well have been a tree associated with pagan worship. Villages often grew around a sacred tree and it is certain that many churches existing today are built on the site of trees which previously have been the centre of pagan worship.

The charter given by Edward the Confessor in 1043 confirming the foundation of a monastery at Coventry gives the earliest known spelling of the place – 'Couaentree'. Among the many variations of the spelling found in documents from then until two centuries later is 'Coventrev' which appears in the Domesday Book.

It seems unlikely, in spite of the rather fragile evidence of a few Roman coins found in excavations here and there, and some pavements of doubtful origin, which are thought by some to have been Roman, that there was any settlement here in Roman times.

Mancetter and Alcester were clearly Roman settlements of sufficient note to have left their names, and it is likely that the Roman network of communications by-passed Coventry.

It is certain that the first significant intervention of Coventry into English history was occasioned by the founding of a convent for nuns in the valley of the Sherbourne. The foundress was Saint Osburga. Who this notable saint was precisely is not clear, though the greater weight of evidence seems to suggest that she was the Abbess of Barking towards the end of the seventh and the beginning of the eighth centuries, and that it was she who founded the early nunnery at Coventry.

The Anglo-Saxon Chronicle records that in 1016, following the revolt of Mercia against King Canute, the nunnery founded by him 'at which at one time the Holy Virgin Osburga was Abbess', was destroyed by 'the traitor Edrie'. When Canute was reasonably secure on the throne of England he set about repairing the damage resulting from the wars, and particularly did he rebuild churches which had been ruined in the wide-spread destruction. It appears that, while the nunnery was restored by King Canute, very shortly after the nuns were driven out and the religious establishment became a monastery by the decision of Leofric, Earl of the Marches. Dugdale's 'History of Warwickshire' records that the dedication ceremony of the new monastery was performed by Archbishop Aedsie of Canterbury on the fourth of the nones of October, 1043, when Abbot Leofwine and twenty-four monks were installed therein. The monastery was dedicated, by authority of Pope Alexander 'to the honour of God, the Virgin Mary, St Peter, St Osburg, and all the Saints'. William of Malmesbury states that 'it was enriched and beautiful with so much gold and silver that the walls seemed too narrow to contain it'. Among the relics was an arm of St Augustine.

The foundation of the monastery in Coventry by Leofric and his wife Godiva, sister to Tharold, Sheriff of Lincolnshire, obviously brought to Coventry all the discipline, purpose and coherence of the Benedictine order, and all the industry and craft which formed part of the monastic life under that order. In fact, it can be said to have marked the beginning of the growth of Coventry as a notable town – 'To the existence of this monastic institution the beginnings of this city's prosperity has been attributed' (Dugdale: 'Warwickshire'). When Leofric died in 1057 at Bromley in Staffordshire his body was brought to Coventry to be buried within the monastery which he had founded.

Leofric and Godiva were great patrons and benefactors of religious houses in Mercia and many great churches owe as much to their benefaction as the Benedictine Monastery at Coventry. Among these are Leominster, Worcester, Evesham, Burton-on-Trent, Ely, Hereford and Stowe.

Leofric's wife, Godiva, was one of the remarkable women of her day. Various records refer to her great beauty, piety and devotion to the service of the Church. She lived until after the Norman Conquest, for the Domesday Book's reference to the village of Madelie in Staffordshire refers to her possessing the manor there after the arrival of William I. There is no certain knowledge of Godiva's burial place, but the general weight of opinion seems to favour the view that she may be buried at Evesham and, because of the disturbed state of the country after 1066, was never moved to join her husband's tomb in the monastery at Coventry.

The original nunnery church founded by St Osburga was probably built of wood, for an early reference to this, quoted by F. Bliss Burbidge in his 'Old Coventry and Lady Godiva', recalls that, 'Wind blew day and night without intermission through the doors and windows of the churches, the fissures of the divisions, the plankings, or the wall'.

The abbey church of Leofric and Godiva was clearly a substantial building. An early reference to it describes 'two porches and a massive, richly-decorated rood beam supporting the shrines' (Burbidge). The chronicler Roger of Wendover tells of its great endowment of wealth, for 'it had not its equal in the whole of England for gold and silver, gems and precious vestments'. Godiva certainly poured her considerable wealth into the firm establishment and beautification of this monastery. Matthew of Westminster (quoted by Burbidge) states that it was built 'out of Godiva's own patrimony, and having established monks in it they endowed it so abundantly with estates and treasures of various kinds that there was not found such a quantity of gold and silver and precious stones in any monastery in England as there was in that monastery at that time'. And again, Ordericus Vitalis describes its great wealth thus: 'The Countess Godiva also a devout lady had contributed all her wealth to the monastery and employed goldsmiths to convert all the gold and silver she possessed into sacred tapestries and crosses and images of saints and other ecclesiastical ornaments of wonderful beauty, which she devoutly distributed'. William of Malmesbury, again quoted by F. B. Burbidge in his 'Old Coventry and Lady Godiva', adds to this picture of magnificence still further when he writes 'Godiva when at the point of death gave a rich chain or collar set with precious stones directing that it should be placed about the neck of the image of the Virgin Mary at Coventry and enjoining that those who came for devotion to the church should say as many prayers as there were stones in the chain'.

The establishment of the Benedictine Monastery at Coventry was the subject of three charters, the following extracts of which give a clear picture of the nature and importance and authority of the monastery. A charter issued by Edward the Confessor addressed to Archbishop Aedsie, who was Archbishop of Canterbury between 1038 and 1047, directs 'that it be from henceforth a house of monks and may they stand in God's grace and in St Mary's and in mine and after St Benedict's Rule and under the guidance of the Abbot. And I will not in any manner consent that any man confiscate or take away their gifts and their alms or that any man have there any charge on any things, or at any time, except the Abbot and the brethren for the needs of the minster. And whoever shall increase these alms with any good the Lord shall give him Heaven's eternal bliss, and whomsoever shall withold them or deprive that minster of anything at any time then let such a one stand in the disfavour of God and of his dear mother and mine.'

The Latin charter of Earl Leofric defines the history of the establishment and dedication of the monastery in the following words: 'In the year of the incarnation of our Lord one thousand and forty-three, I, Earl Leofric, by the counsel and advice of King Edward and Pope Alexander, who sent to me his letter written below with a seal, and by the testimony of other devout men, laymen as well as churchmen, have caused the Church of Coventry to be dedicated in honour of God and St Mary his mother, of St Peter the Apostle, of St Osburga the Virgin, and all saints'. This charter then conveys to the monastery twenty-four towns 'to the Church for the service of God and for the food and clothing of the Abbot and monks serving God in the same place'. The towns so conveyed are those known today as Honington, Newnham, Chadshunt, Bishops Itchington, Ufton, Southam, Grandborough, Birdingbury, Marston, Hardwick, Wasperton, Chesterton, Southam in Gloucestershire, Ryton, Marston in Gloucester, Salwarp in Worcestershire, Eaton in Chester, Kilsby and Winwick in Northamptonshire, Burbage, Barwell, Packington and Potters Marston in Leicester. 'And these lands I have given to the monastery with sac and soc and toll and team with the liberties and customs in every place.'

King Edward wrote thus to the Abbot of Coventry in 1043: 'I, King Edward, greet in friendship my bishops, earls, and all my ministers in those counties where Leofric the abbat in Coventry has lands. And I declare to you that I wish that he may be entitled to his sac and his soc, and toll and team, over his land and over his men within towns and without as fully and completely as Earl Leofric had originally. And I will not suffer any man to do him wrong in anything'. This is the oldest known genuine Coventry ecclesiastical document and was discovered in 1951 by Miss F. E. Harmer.

The Latin confirmation of the original charter of King

Edward the Confessor, apparently copied in the fifteenth century from an original, though suspected of some alteration at the time of the copying, contains the command of Edward the Confessor, 'That all things that relate to the Church be wholly free, lands cultivated and uncultivated, with outgoings and rents of the aforesaid places, and manors, churches, cemeteries, tithes, revenues and services due, offerings, altar lights and hearing of suits, correction of things ecclesiastical or lay, and whatsoever else hath been confirmed upon that place, we grant again freely and confirm forever'. The Latin version of the original charter contains also a quotation from a letter, apparently written by the Pope Alexander at the time of the granting of the charter, in which the Pope enjoins, 'Let the brethren of the same place have the power of choosing fit persons as abbots or deans in succession from amongst themselves, or from any assembly they may choose; and we forbid that they be hindered by apostolic authority'. Bliss Burbidge's 'Old Coventry and Lady Godiva' records these charters in great detail and is cautious about their absolute accuracy. Nonetheless, the quotations from that admirable book recorded above serve to convey an impression of a monastery established under the highest authority in the kingdom, and holding status and power to mark it as a centre of influence in the England of the eleventh and twelfth centuries.

The church which was restored by Canute as a nunnery and the subject of the charter of 1043 as a monastery, the first abbot of which was Leofwine, was enormously enlarged between that

Plan of the Benedictine Priory in relation to the present Cathedral

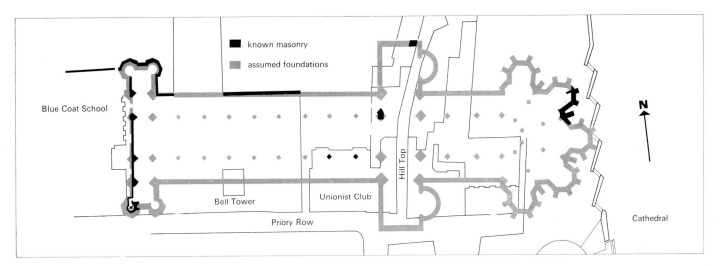

Painting of the interior of St Michael's Church by David Gee, in the Herbert Art Gallery

Painting of Coventry from the north-east, showing Christ Church, St Michael's and Holy Trinity spire, c. 1700, in the Herbert Art Gallery

date and about 1220. The building apparently started soon after 1100 and the most continuous period of building occupied about eighty years. At its completion it must have been one of the most majestic sights of mediaeval England. Standing on the hill at the centre of Coventry, on the eastern slope of which the new Cathedral now stands, was a building of approximately 450 feet in length with a breadth at its west end estimated at from 136 to 145 feet. The traveller approaching Coventry from the north would have seen a view of the central hill which must have been utterly breathtaking. Lying west to east along the northern slope of the hill was this great and magnificent Cathedral with a great central tower and two towers standing at the north-west and south-west of the west front, apparently at the entrance to each transept. Behind this magnificent Cathedral, slightly higher up on the hill, was the glorious parish church of St Michael with its lofty spire exceeding 300 feet, and the beautiful parish church of Holy Trinity slightly to westward.

While the main body of the Cathedral appears to have been completed by about 1220, there obviously was some continual activity during the next three centuries and various records recall building activity in 1409 and in 1462.

The five hundred years' life of the monastery at Coventry was by no means uniformly peaceful. Hostility between the prior and the earl led to continual friction. The opposition of bishops, notably Bishop Robert Delimesi, who seems to have been motivated by covetousness, seriously hampered the progress of the monastery. William of Malmesbury wrote: 'This Robert, Bishop of the Diocese, eagerly took possession of in a totally unepiscopal fashion, stealing the treasures of the church in order to fill the hands of the King, destroy the vigilance of the Pope, and satisfy the greed of the Romans. During the many years he continued there he gave no sign of worth whatever, for instead of restoring the sagging roofs he wasted the sacred treasures, became guilty of peculation and might have been convicted of improper exactions had an accuser been forthcoming. He fed the monks on inferior victuals and failed to stimulate in them a love of their calling, and allowed them to reach only a low degree of learning lest it should make them delicate by fine living or severity of rule or depth of learning encourage them to offer opposition.'

The twelfth century marked an invasion by Sir Robert Marmion of Tamworth in his attack against his enemy the Earl

*Painting of Coventry Cathedral and Holy Trinity
from the north-east, 1830, by David Gee,
in the Herbert Art Gallery.
This shows Priory Street and what is now the site of
the new Cathedral*

of Chester. In 1184 Hugh de Nonant was made Bishop of Coventry, described as 'crafty, bold and shameless'. He had an inveterate hatred of monks, which he vented on the monks of Coventry. Contention broke out between the monks of Coventry and the canons of Lichfield, which did not make for harmonious living, nor did the possession by the monks of the liberties of the townsfolk of Coventry make for harmony between the monastery and the town. The townsfolk, who were increasingly involved in the growing craft and activity of the town, not without the encouragement of the earl, were in a constant state of opposition to the prior and encroached upon the prior's powers and possessions whenever opportunity offered.

While the Coventry monastery was not a particularly large one, having only twenty-four monks within it, it was nonethe-

less very prosperous. Dugdale records that the income of the monastery in 1538 when Henry VIII ordered its dissolution was £731 19s 5d. The monastery (with its possessions) was granted in 1545 to Sir Ralph Sadler, who sold it to one John Hales. Hales was a cripple, his foot having been injured when his dagger fell in front of him while he was running, and he stepped on it, being pierced right through his foot by it. Hales turned some of the domestic quarters of the monastery into a private residence, where, incidentally, he entertained Queen Elizabeth. In 1717 his descendant sold the property to John, Duke of Montague, who sold it to Samuel Hill of Shenstone Park, Staffordshire. It later passed to Mr Smith, a clergyman of Aspley in Bedfordshire, who sold it in 1801 'to the directors of the poor of this City'. It rapidly fell into decay and now virtually nothing remains.

The utter destruction of this great and glorious monastery seems to imply a greed, avarice and wanton destruction which makes dreadful imagining.

The lead from the great Cathedral Church, estimated to be worth the very great sum of £647, was soon removed, and it did not take long before the beautiful walls crumbled or were pulled down so that very soon the site of the great monastery became a stone quarry from which citizens removed stones for the foundations of houses and bridges – evidence of which is still to be found here and there in the city, even after the great destruction of the war of 1939-45.

The foundations of some of the eastward buttresses are carefully preserved near the entrance to the present Cathedral Refectory, and here and there in Holy Trinity churchyard evidence can be found of the original walls, though most of the remains have either been covered up by other buildings or since destroyed.

Towards the end of the reign of Henry VIII an Act was passed which decided 'that the Dean and Chapter of Lichfield should be forever the entire and sole Chapter of the Bishopric of Coventry and Lichfield'. The Bishops of the diocese signed themselves 'Coventry and Lichfield' until the Restoration, when precedence in title was given to Lichfield on account of the support by the latter of the Royalist cause in the Civil War. 'Lichfield and Coventry' it remained until Coventry was joined to the diocese of Worcester, from which it was taken in 1918 when the present diocese of Coventry was created, and the ancient parish church of St Michael became the second Cathedral of Coventry

The Religious Plays of Coventry

The pageants or religious mystery plays of Coventry were as famous in their day as those of York and Chester. The quality of the plays which survive make one aware of the great loss resulting from the failure to preserve either the scripts or the traditions of these plays.

Dugdale speaks of the part played by the Grey Friars of Coventry in directing the plays which were performed under the patronage of the Guilds:

'The Grey Friars of Coventry were celebrated for certain mystical exhibitions termed Corpus Christi Plays, from the day on which they were annually performed, and founded upon some story, by then deemed sacred. They are said to have presented their pageants from high and portable theatres, placed in the most open and advantageous part of the City. It was customary to announce the subject in a sort of prologue, by a person called Vexillator, who is supposed to have carried a flag upon which was painted the subject of the day–and to have explained to the audience the nature and history of the drama which was to be submitted to their inspection.'

The mystery plays of Coventry were normally performed after the public procession held on Corpus Christi Day. To quote from F. Bliss Burbidge: 'The accounts of the Carpenters' Company show that this procession started soon after breakfast at an early hour, probably to allow time for the plays which occupied the rest of the day. Apparently, the members of the craft companies headed the assembly, proceeding two by two in their proper liveries. The order, according to the Coventry Leet Book was: Fishers and Cooks; Bakers and Millers; Butchers; Whittawers and Glovers; Pinners, Tylers and Wrights; Barkers; Corvisers; Smiths, Weavers; Wiredrawers; Cardmakers; Saddlers, Painters, and Masons; Girdlers; Taylors, Walkers and Shearmen; Dysters; Drapers; Mercers. These worthies were preceded by their torchbearers and attended by their journeymen, the accounts of the Dyers Company showing that the torchbearers wore straw hats and surplices. From the fact that the Mercers came last in order, it is suggested that they were given the honourable position of immediately preceding the Host.'

It was after the procession, in which the mayor, civic dignitaries and church leaders took part, that the mystery plays were enacted. The plays were clearly of a liturgical character, as indeed most plays of this period were under the guidance of the Church. Although it is known that the plays were acted before the end of the twelfth century, they do not appear to have become firmly established in English history until the end of the fourteenth century. The material of the plays was essentially religious and its teaching was clearly under the control of religious guidance, though the subsequent development of these plays fell more and more into the hands of the guilds themselves.

Only two of the plays included in the Coventry Corpus Christi pageant are extant.

The list of plays and the guilds which performed them is summarised in Burbidge's 'Old Coventry and Lady Godiva' as follows:

'SHEARMEN AND TAYLORS The Annunciation. Joseph's Doubt. Journey to Bethlehem. The Nativity. Angels and Shepherds. Herod and the Wise Men. The Flight to Egypt. The Slaughter of the Innocents.

'WEAVERS Presentation in the Temple. Christ and the Elders.

'MERCERS The Assumption.

'SMITHS Trial and Crucifixion. Death of Judas.

'PINNERS AND NEEDLERS Descent from the Cross (in 1414).

'COOPERS Descent from the Cross (in 1547).

'CARDMAKERS AND CAPPERS Harrowing of Hell. The Resurrection. "Whom seek ye?".

'CAPPERS Castle of Emaus (in 1540).

'DRAPERS Doomsday.'

The mystery plays were performed on movable stages, usually mounted on wheels. Sketches which exist show that the action on these constricted stages took place on an upper level, which was open to view on all sides, while the lower part acted as a dressing-room to hide the actors. The draping of the whole movable stage gave opportunities which, from such records as survive, were evidently taken to display the full pageantry associated with the sponsoring guild.

The narrow streets of a mediaeval town could have given

Revival of the Coventry mystery plays, supplemented into a full sequence, performed in the ruins of the old Cathedral by members of the Theatre Guild of Coventry in 1962 and 1964

The Creation

The Annunciation

The Woman taken in Adultery

The Temptation

The Renunciation of the Devil by Mary Magdalen

The Crucifixion

Religious drama productions in the new Cathedral

Raising of Lazarus

Prodigal Son

Black Nativity

True Misterie of the Passion

The Site, a Porch Play

Waiting for Godot

B

The Business of Good Government

The Book of Job

Exit the King

very little scope for the assembling of large crowds and it is likely that the pageant was performed over a period of days in the various wards of the town. The wards remain today named, as they were then; Gosford, Jordan Well, Much Park, Bayley Lane, Earl Street, Broadgate, Smithford Street, Spon Street, Cross Cheaping and Bishop Street.

In 1457 the Coventry pageant was honoured by a visit from Queen Margaret and an extract from the Leet Book for May 31st, 1457, quoted by Burbidge, records: 'On Corpus Christi even at night then next ensuing came the Queen Margaret from Kenilworth to Coventry; at which time she would not be met, but came privilly to see the play there on the morrow, and she saw them all the pageants played except Doomsday, which might not be played for lack of day. And she lodged at Richard Woods's, the grocer, where Richard Sharp sometime dwelled, and there all the plays were first played.'

Performance of a mystery play c. 1500

Trade and Industry in Coventry

By the middle of the thirteenth century the wool trade was highly developed in the Midlands and its centre was at Leicester. The Coventry monks, together with the neighbouring Cistercian abbeys of Coombe and Stoneleigh, specialised in the breeding of sheep and the marketing of their wool. It was natural, therefore, that a growing town like Coventry should soon develop a by-product of this wool trade, and the Coventry weavers were among the first to establish themselves as an efficient and progressive craft guild. Mr Levi Fox in his book 'Coventry's Heritage' collects a few names at the beginning of the fourteenth century which show the range of some of the citizens of Coventry engaged in this trade: Agnes Staunford, 'thredmaker'; Adam Heton, 'deyster'; John Blomley, 'draper'; Multon, 'mercator'; Joan the daughter of William, 'the hosier'; Elena Cardemaker, 'wool comber'; William Kyng, 'wevere'.

The making of wool into cloth became Coventry's chief industry until the beginning of Tudor times, and its excellence earned it a reputation throughout Europe. A constant coming and going of trade from Coventry to Bristol conveyed the products of the Coventry homesteads to places as far as the Baltic ports, eastern Europe and the Middle East.

'True as Coventry blue' is a tribute to the excellence of dyes used for the treatment of the cloth woven.

The making of caps and gloves were natural developments of this early trade. Fullers, felt makers and drapers were equally inevitable results of its growth.

The whole weaving industry was very highly organised, according to its own processes or crafts, each of which was organised into its own guild or merchant company, controlled by rules which were approved by the governing body of the city called the 'Court Leet'. The training of apprentices and the protection of the trade from outside competition was carefully safeguarded by these guilds. Obviously at the height of the prosperity of the industry the guilds grew increasingly powerful. In St Michael's parish church they established their membership of the community as articulated by this great parish church, and also their loyalty to the church by establishing in St Michael's chapels set aside for the devotion of the particular guild under whose patronage the chapel was made. So in St Michael's, up to its destruction in 1940, there existed chapels for the Cappers Guild, the Dyers, the Weavers, the Grocers and the Smiths.

A silk book mark woven in Coventry in 1838. Part of the collection of silk pictures in the Herbert Museum

A early Rudge Whitworth bicycle

Daimler motor car c. 1897

A Coventry watchmaker

One of the most sustained characteristics of Coventry's industry has been its unfailing resilience. It has at no time tied itself inextricably to one industry and risked its fortunes on the rise or fall of that industry's prosperity. So from the time of its industrial growth, beginning in the simple society of 1200 and going on to the Industrial Revolution, other crafts besides those associated with weaving and drapery developed – notably clocks, watches, instrument-making, working in brass, pewter and iron, and leather. By the middle of the fifteenth century the leather trade was flourishing and well-established. Excavations in modern Coventry have revealed harnesses and sheaths, and broad-toed shoes, in a considerable quantity, dating before the Reformation. Glass-making was well established in Coventry by the beginning of the fifteenth century and is, in fact, mentioned as early as 1302. One of the famous glaziers of his day was John Thornton, some of whose work is still in existence in the stained glass which was removed from the apse of St Michael's and is being restored to places here and there in the new Cathedral. This John Thornton was responsible for the glazing of the large east window of York Minster.

The cloth and cap trades declined during the seventeenth century but with its inevitable resilience Coventry found new prosperity in the making of clocks, watches and instruments. By the middle of the eighteenth century and the beginning of the nineteenth, the watch trade had developed very considerably and Coventry was one of the principal centres of this industry in Britain. By 1861 the trade employed over 2,000 people.

The concentration of so much skill in precision working made Coventry a natural place for the great move forward in mechanical engineering at the end of the nineteenth century. The making of the first bicycle in Coventry established this industry firmly in the city and made the rapid development of other forms of mechanical transport a natural development from the bicycle.

The First World War, occurring as it did early in the life of the motor-car and aeroplane, made demands upon the existing industry of Coventry in such a way as to cause the industrial life of the city to take a very great step forward, and during the 1914-18 war the population very nearly doubled. Precisely the same thing occurred during the Second World War, when

another 100,000 people were added to the population during the war and the ten years which followed it, to bring Coventry to its 1961 population of about 320,000. But during this period the range of industry in Coventry developed so widely that there are now more than four hundred separate industries in the city, spread over so wide a range of activities that the same historic resilience preserves for Coventry an assurance of prosperity which concentration in any one particular industry to the exclusion of others would not give it.

Interior of a modern Coventry car factory

Rayon manufacture

An aircraft assembly line

High precision tool-making
with tolerances to $+.00005''$, $-.00005''$

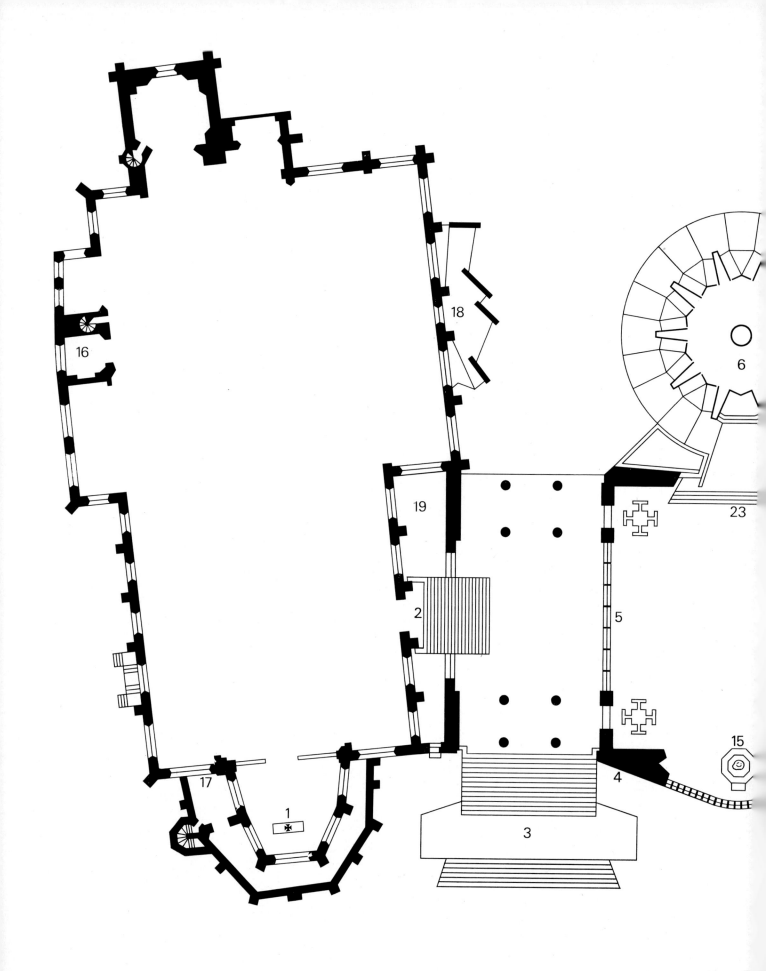

plan of the Cathedral

1 Altar and charred cross, Old Cathedral
2 The Queen's Steps leading from the Ruins to the Porch
    of the New Cathedral (site of Porch Plays)
3 St Michael's Steps
4 St Michael and the Devil
5 West Screen of the Cathedral – The Hutton Screen
6 The Chapel of Unity
7 The Bishop's Throne
8 Tablets of the Word
9 The Nave
10 The Lectern
11 The High Altar
12 The Lady Chapel
13 The Chapel of Christ in Gethsemane
14 The Chapel of Christ the Servant
15 The Font

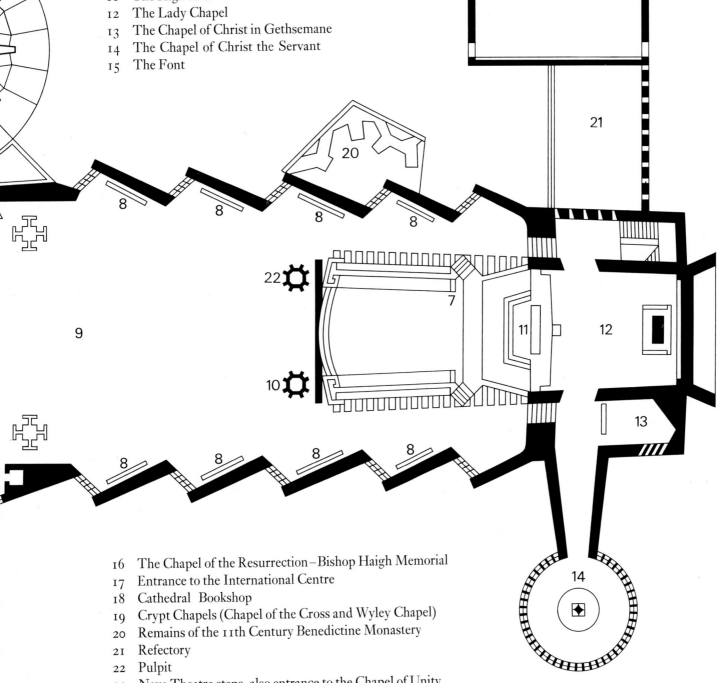

16 The Chapel of the Resurrection – Bishop Haigh Memorial
17 Entrance to the International Centre
18 Cathedral Bookshop
19 Crypt Chapels (Chapel of the Cross and Wyley Chapel)
20 Remains of the 11th Century Benedictine Monastery
21 Refectory
22 Pulpit
23 Nave Theatre steps, also entrance to the Chapel of Unity

A Tour of Coventry Cathedral

The true sequence of a visit to Coventry Cathedral should be through the sequence of its history. The starting point is the tallest spire on the skyline, approached from Broadgate by such colourful names as Pepper Lane, Hay Lane, Bayley Lane, Cuckoo Lane or Priory Row. These names throw one's mind back immediately to mediaeval Coventry with the priory dominating the hill top. Indeed the attractive pedestrian way called 'Hill Top' now goes very nearly across the same path as one would have walked if one had walked across the old priory of St Mary's from one transept to the other. Nestling round the old Cathedral, Holy Trinity and St Michael's churches in mediaeval Coventry would have been some of the merchants' stores and exchanges. The entrance to the Cathedral through the western approach brings one into the ruins under the shadow of the soaring 310 feet high spire with its massive tower base, restored in the 1870s, surmounted by an octagonal tower from which grows the graceful Gothic spire.

A story is told that during the 1939-45 war, soon after the bombing of Coventry, when many buildings were cracked, broken or leaning, the Royal Engineers put explosives to these buildings to blow them up in the interests of safety. It is said that an enthusiastic lieutenant with his party took a bearing on the spire, found it was 5 feet out of true, and set about preparing to blow it up. Soon after starting this fearsome operation a senior officer passing by asked the lieutenant what he was about and, when told, remarked dryly that he would not bother very much if he were the lieutenant because it had been 5 feet out of true for a hundred years. So the spire survives virtually untouched, for the bombs which destroyed St Michael's Church in 1940 were fire bombs and not high explosives.

At any time of the year the visitor will be blown by the north wind on entering the great west door. This is a trick of the wind whistling around the surrounding buildings from whichever direction it may come. It is inevitable that a legend should have grown out of this, and the legend is that in distant times the Devil and the North Wind were passing through Coventry and the Devil said to the North Wind 'Wait here a moment while I go in': he has never come out, being held captive inside, and the North Wind still waits!

Passing into the Cathedral ruins one is overwhelmed immediately by a sense of dignity and peace. At the centre of the bustling city of Coventry there stands this place of quietness in which many people regularly find comfort, and use the benches provided by many persons and local bodies who wish to contribute something worthwhile to the amenities of their city. In the distance at the east end the heart of the whole conception and ministry of Coventry Cathedral rivets the attention of the visitor. But before reaching that point of meditation there is much to see about one. On the left is the open-air stage, built soon after the war had ended, for the performance of revived mystery plays. It now forms an important part of the whole drama project, based on Coventry Cathedral, with the obvious limitations of the English weather. Around the walls are two different series of wall plaques. One series marks the positions in the Cathedral of some of the old guild chapels—the Smiths, the Cappers, the Dyers, the Grocers. Hard by the old Cappers Chapel and above the Chapel of the Resurrection, restored as a memorial to Bishop Mervyn Haigh, who was Bishop at the time of the destruction of the Cathedral in 1940, is the Cappers Room, restored by the Cappers Guild as an annual meeting place, and for two and a half years, until February 1963, used as the Coventry studio of the British Broadcasting Corporation, which now is housed in the undercroft of the Cathedral itself.

The second series of wall plaques are known as the Hallowing Places. Here in a sequence of well-phrased prayers are invitations to pray for blessings upon home and family, upon sufferers, upon industry and commerce, and upon our leisure.

It may be that by this time the clock will have struck and, if

*April, 1964. The Charred Cross was sent to America
to be at the centre of meditation in the Protestant Pavilion in the
World Fair in New York*

*The British Broadcasting Corporation studio in Coventry
Cathedral*

it is the hour for the playing of it, the striking of the hour will have been followed by the playing of one or other of the sequence of hymn tunes which have become a nostalgic part of the music of the centre of this city. There are fourteen fine bells in the tower, but because of the danger of vibration to the spire the bells have not been properly rung for nearly a century. From time to time during the year peals are electronically played, in obedience to requests made by citizens of Coventry during the past centuries that on important anniversaries in the donor's life a peal should be played.

From the balustrade of the tower about 150 feet high, set as it is at the highest point of the hill, is one of the most commanding views of Coventry and the country round about.

Standing before the sanctuary of the ruins the visitor is

compelled to profound meditation. The walls of the sanctuary still bear the scars of destruction and the stains of molten lead which boiled when the Cathedral burned. Central to the sanctuary is the stone altar table fashioned out of broken stones gathered after the destruction. It is surmounted by one of the most significant crosses in Christendom, the famous Charred Cross of Coventry. Soon after the destruction of the Cathedral a workman gathered two of the remains of the mediaeval oak beams which had framed the ceiling of the Cathedral, fastened them together with rough wire and fixed them in an old refuse bin within which the cross was held in position by builders' sand. The Charred Cross survived storm and tempest for twenty years before it showed signs of deterioration. Then it was taken down for the first time and sprayed under pressure with liquid amber and so fossilised and made secure for all time. In 1963 this famous cross of Christian reconciliation journeyed to America to be the central exhibit in the Protestant and Orthodox Pavilion of the New York World's Fair, and during its absence it was replaced by an exact replica made by craftsmen in Stratford-on-Avon.

On the altar table itself is another world-famous cross, the Coventry Cross of Nails. When the roof of St Michael's burned, the nails, which were hand-forged in the fourteenth century and driven in to hold the oak beams together, were spread over the rubble. By the inspiration of a priest in the diocese and a young student who subsequently became a priest and joined the staff of the Cathedral, three nails were fastened together in the form of a cross, and so was born the Cross of Nails. In this form it has become the symbol of Coventry's international Christian ministry and has found its way to centres all over the world with which the ministry of Coventry Cathedral has tried to establish a creative relationship, leading to the interchange of minds and regular and growing visits. Among these centres of creative exchange are East and West Berlin, Oslo, Hamburg, Münster, Kiel, Paris, Montreal, New York, Washington, Alabama, South Africa, Australia, New Zealand, Tanganyika and Kenya.

There are those who misunderstand the intention of the inscription 'Father Forgive'. In order to make it perfectly clear that this prayer quoted from Calvary itself acknowledges the universality of human guilt, one of the results of which is the massive tragedy of war, the Coventry Cathedral litany of reconciliation has been printed on a plaque and stands before the altar, inviting those who look at it to share in its prayer. This litany is printed in many languages and is repeated in the sanctuary every Friday at noon.

'ALL HAVE SINNED AND COME SHORT OF THE GLORY OF GOD.'

THE HATRED WHICH DIVIDES NATION FROM NATION, RACE FROM RACE, CLASS FROM CLASS,

FATHER, FORGIVE.

THE COVETOUS DESIRES OF MEN AND NATIONS TO POSSESS WHAT IS NOT THEIR OWN,

FATHER, FORGIVE.

THE GREED WHICH EXPLOITS THE LABOURS OF MEN AND LAYS WASTE THE EARTH,

FATHER, FORGIVE.

OUR ENVY OF THE WELFARE AND HAPPINESS OF OTHERS,

FATHER, FORGIVE.

OUR INDIFFERENCE TO THE PLIGHT OF THE HOMELESS AND THE REFUGEE,

FATHER, FORGIVE.

THE LUST WHICH USES FOR IGNOBLE ENDS THE BODIES OF MEN AND WOMEN,

FATHER, FORGIVE.

THE PRIDE WHICH LEADS US TO TRUST IN OURSELVES, AND NOT IN GOD,

FATHER, FORGIVE.

'BE KIND TO ONE ANOTHER, TENDER-HEARTED, FORGIVING ONE ANOTHER,

AS GOD IN CHRIST FORGAVE YOU'

The German warden of the International Centre with a visitor from India

A mural in the International Centre showing the symbol of 'Aktion Sühnezeichen' – made by Fritz Kühn of East Berlin and presented by the East German Churches

In October, 1961, sixteen young Germans representing 'Aktion Sühnezeichen' – 'Operation Reconciliation' – came to live at the Cathedral for six months to build the International Centre. It is significantly appropriate that this Centre should embrace the sanctuary of reconciliation in the ruins, and the work of the German team consisted of a restoration of the old vestries which formed a semi-circle around the sanctuary. The Centre now includes a reception room, a lounge, a small canteen, an international library and a small room for quiet and meditation. Tens of thousands of foreign visitors enter the Centre every year.

At the eastern end of the nave of the ruins are two tombs. One is that of Bishop Yeatman-Biggs, who was Bishop of Coventry when the Diocese of Coventry was reformed in 1918. The other, on the south side of the nave, is that of Bishop Neville Gorton, who became Bishop of Coventry after the translation of Bishop Mervyn Haigh to the Diocese of Winchester, having previously been headmaster of Blundells School. It was Bishop Gorton who, together with the then provost, the Very Reverend R. T. Howard, planned the early design of the new Cathedral.

The visitor now has approached the new Cathedral in the correct historical and theological sequence, for the sanctuary of the ruins is the heart of Coventry Cathedral. It was from this point that Sir Basil Spence, the Cathedral architect, conceived the shape and general outline of the new Cathedral.

When it was decided that the new Cathedral should be begun, Sir Giles Gilbert-Scott was commissioned to produce a

The design by Sir Giles Gilbert-Scott
for the new Cathedral

A Coventry cross of nails presented to the Benedictine Monastery at Ottobeuren, Germany

design, which he did in a beautiful Gothic idiom. Gilbert-Scott's Cathedral had a central altar, a feature which was well ahead of liturgical thinking at that time. For various reasons this design was not eventually accepted, and Sir Giles Gilbert-Scott very graciously accepted the decision and withdrew.

The design of the new Cathedral was then thrown open to competition, and this was won by Mr, later Sir, Basil Spence. Sir Basil Spence records his own experience of the controversy which his design aroused, a controversy in which all those who were interested in the new Cathedral shared, some with sympathy, some in opposition. That Sir Basil Spence's design was well ahead of ecclesiastical architectural thinking at the time is as obvious still as it was then, but that his design was absolutely right is the opinion of the great majority of those who visit the Cathedral. Sir Basil Spence is the first to acknowledge that his Cathedral design is not radically modern, but that basically its lines are traditional and that it combines, as Christianity always should, the deep insights of the old with the fresh challenges of the new.

The Reconstruction Committee appointed by the Cathedral Council at all times showed itself to be courageous and far-sighted, and supported Sir Basil Spence in the selection of new and vigorous artists in the adornment of the new Cathedral.

The approach to the Cathedral from the ruins leads through the Queen's Arch, down the Queen's Steps, into the great porch. From the top of the Queen's Steps one can see through the great west screen of clear glass the full sweep of the new Cathedral nave, culminating in the massive altar table and the great tapestry behind it. The Queen's Steps are so called because in 1956 when Her Majesty Queen Elizabeth II laid the foundation stone it was under the arch at the top of these steps that she approached the place for the laying of the stone. It was also through this arch and down these steps that Her Majesty, Princess Margaret, the Earl of Snowdon and a very great distinguished international company processed to the consecration of the new Cathedral on 25th May, 1962.

The great west screen of clear glass is the design and execution of Mr John Hutton. The intention here is to suggest that it is through history and an interpretation of history, and through the witness and often the suffering of faithful representatives of God through that history that one gets a true perspective of the present and the future. At the top of the

*The great west screen designed and executed
by John Hutton*

An engraved flying angel from the west screen

Detail of St Alban in the west screen

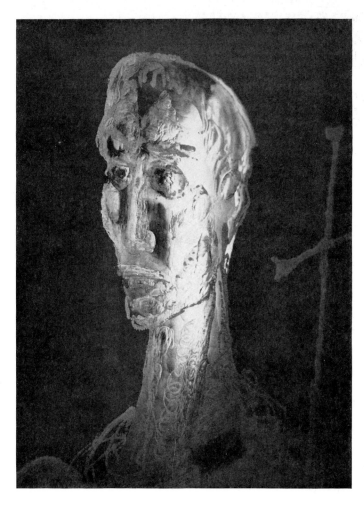

design is a row of Old Testament patriarchs and prophets. The next row of historic figures represents leading figures from the New Testament. The third row of identifiable figures is a selection of English saints, and the lowest row of all is a selection of saints particularly associated with the Midlands and the old Kingdom of Mercia. Separating these rows of historic figures are rows of angels depicted as heavenly creatures expressing triumph and joy.

The great porch serves many purposes. First, obviously, it is the link between the old and the new, declaring that the whole Cathedral is one, with the new growing out of the old. Secondly, it serves as a public pedestrian way at a significant meeting of the ways in the centre of Coventry. Those on their way from the coach station to the Broadgate, or from the shopping centre to the Lanchester College of Technology pass regularly through the Cathedral itself. It is an acknowledgment of this fact which, among other reasons, has justified the opening by a clear glass screen of the activities inside the Cathedral to the view of all those who pass outside it. Thirdly, the porch serves as a meeting place for drama presentations in the summer, and the Coventry Cathedral porch plays have earned a wide reputation.

As one approaches the new Cathedral one enters the left door to pass around the aisles through the Lady Chapel on what has become the pilgrims' way. In order to make it very clear that the Cathedral is before all else a House of Prayer the whole of the centre of the nave is regularly kept clear for those who wish to kneel or sit quietly, or to pray.

On entering the Cathedral, one's eyes are turned irresistibly to the right, particularly in the morning when the sun shines from the east. Here is the great symphony of colour which is the Baptistry Window. The whole window was designed by Sir Basil Spence and the stained glass was designed by Mr John Piper and made by Mr Patrick Reyntiens. The overall symbolism of this window is of light breaking through darkness, or the light of truth breaking through the conflicts and confusions of the world. The opinion of most is that this is a crowning glory of Coventry Cathedral.

On the left, as one goes along the aisle, is the stage of the nave theatre. This is the third of the areas where the Coventry drama department presents its plays and with the audience seated laterally across the Cathedral, facing this stage, plays can be performed to an audience of six hundred people. The stage serves also as the principal entrance to the Chapel of Unity. This chapel is under the control of a joint council of the representative leaders of the Christian denominations of the city. It is clad on its outside in Westmorland slate, which contrasts with the pink sandstone of the main building. The floor is the work of the distinguished artist Mr Einar Forseth of Sweden, and was the gift of the Swedish people, led in their donations by Their Majesties the King and Queen of Sweden. The design has at its centre the dove, as the symbol of the Holy Spirit, and it is surrounded by symbols of the four evangelists and representations of the five continents, together with smaller designs of classical Christian symbols. The windows in the Chapel of Unity were made by Margaret Traherne and are a beautiful sequence of colour patterns which cast exciting lighting effects on the marble floor when the sun shines through them. These windows were paid for by a gift from the German Church presented by the late President Theodor Heuss on his official visit to England in October, 1958.

Confronting the visitor on the journey down the aisle are the Tablets of the Word. These Tablets of the Word record some of the great and significant texts of the Christian faith, texts which were repeated by the early Christians in the spread of their faith. Some of the Tablets contain also early Christian symbols, as found on the walls of the catacombs under Rome. They have been carved in asymmetrical letters to suggest primitive carving, which in turn is a reminder of the early Christian origin of these texts, and also to suggest that they

Left : The pedestrian way beneath
the porch cross

The inscription at the nave
entrance

The Baptistry Window and Bethlehem Font

Above right: the interior of the Chapel of Unity
Below: the mosaic floor, gift of the people of Sweden, designed by Einar Forseth

were made by the hand of a man and not by a machine. The man, in fact, who designed and made them was Mr Ralph Beyer, a German sculptor who subsequently lived in England.

Approaching the choir, one is aware of the unusual design of the canopy over the choir stalls. Here is the first of three representations of the Crown of Thorns, and the suggestion here is made that as one approaches the full gift of God's grace, represented by the sacrament of the Holy Communion at the altar, one must journey through the problems and the conflicts and the sufferings of life. Over the Bishop's Throne is a mitre, and over the Provost's Stall is a flame representing the Holy Spirit; these were the work of Elizabeth Frink, who also designed the powerful eagle on the lectern. Before going through

the tunnel under one half of the organ, one gains one's first overall impression of the nave windows. These ten windows are each 70 feet high. They are the work of three men: Lawrence Lee, Geoffrey Clarke and Keith New.

The orientation of the ten great windows of Coventry Cathedral southwards to form the angled window recesses was made necessary by the northward facing position of the Cathedral itself. In a church facing east in the traditional way the southern walls faced the southern arc of the sun and enabled adequate light to enter the church. The orientation of the Cathedral windows southward enables both morning and afternoon sun to pour light through the beautiful colours of the windows to give light to the nave.

The lectern eagle designed by Elizabeth Frink

The windows were designed in a sequence of colour to give emphasis to the focal point of worship – the sanctuary and its massive altar – by placing in the final pair glass capable of shedding on the sanctuary the maximum amount of light. This is further emphasised by making the pair of windows immediately preceding this pair dark, by the use of deep blue and purple glass.

On entering the Cathedral the ten windows are hidden, apart from the kaleidoscope of colour thrown by the sun in rays either on the white walls which face the viewer, and which hold the great Tablets of the Word, or on the black marble floor of the aisles, where the colour is reflected as in deep, still pools of water.

The windows, in their colour and design, contain suggestions of the answers to the two great quests which the Christian religion is designed to unfold – the truth about God, and the truth about Man, and the relationship between them. The fact that the whole composite picture is only to be seen from the altar position suggests that only by full membership of the Church, beginning at the font, and – through all the instruction and discipline of the Church – reaching its fulfilment at the altar, can these truths be, at least initially, understood.

Standing then at the Altar, or behind it in the Lady Chapel, and looking down to the entrance, the first impression is that the windows – as far as their colour is concerned – are designed in pairs. Further reflection will reveal that this pairing of the windows is true also of their design. It is as pairs that the windows must be interpreted and understood.

Beginnings – the first pair, numbers 1 and 2, Green

(1) The emergence of life in all its freshness, sparkling in a suggestion of the uninhibited joy of new creation. New shoots tell of the creation of the natural order, and – in analogy – of the freshness and uninhibited joy of birth and childhood. This window is the gift of the children of the schools of Coventry.

(2) The highest order of God's creation is Man, in whom God has placed the responsibility of administering His world. The response of Man to this charge is – at its best – vision and idealism. Man as a creator reflects God the Creator most perfectly when he is a member of a family. The growth of Man from his creation, and his difficult journey through experience to manhood is the theme of this window. At the base of the

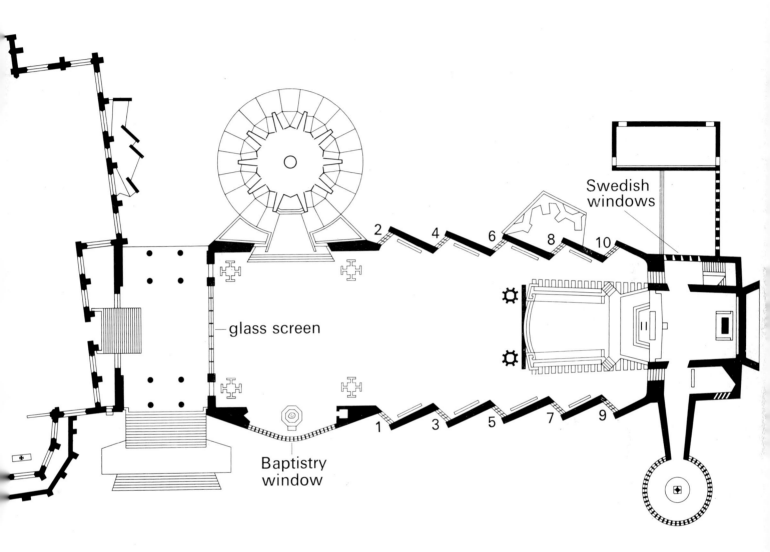

glass screen

Swedish windows

Baptistry window

2 4 6 8 10

1 3 5 7 9

window is the landscape of the earth from which Man comes: symbols of spring, and the pain of birth, of fertility, of baptism and the family group take the eye upwards till the adolescent springs away on his own, ascending the tree of knowledge to the spinning wheel of fortune under a golden cloud at the top.

God's Intervention—the second pair, numbers 3 and 4, Red

(3) Man's life is entered by God. God's intervention in Man's life is suggested by a burst of light at the centre; it is dramatic, 'explosive', sending rays of light to the four corners. This window traces in symbolism Man's historic response to God's intervention. At the base, male and female figures lie prone

under a religion dominated by elemental forces of nature. Symbols rise of the God of the Sun and the Key of the Nile to typify this. A pomegranate (the Word or the Seed) produces a tree from which grows the special religion of the Jews. The Exodus is symbolised. After passing through the river the great conceptions of the Old Testament appear: (a) The Law–the tablets of stone; (b) The Messiah–the Serpent lifted up in the wilderness; (c) Sacrifice–the ram caught in a bush; (d) The Leading of God–the pillar of fire.

Above this is the mystery of God, symbolised by the withdrawal within the Tabernacle, and the closed eye of God. The Old Testament Faith is summed up in the seven-branched candlestick, from the central flame of which the Word grows, but within the larger shape, symbolising the Virgin Mary. The symbols of the Incarnation are those of Earth (point ascending to Heaven) and Heaven (point descending to Earth). The open eyes in the symbol of the Word show the revealed will of God through the Incarnation.

The Coventry Cross within the glory represents the life and passion of Christ and from this grows the New Testament. The new faith is an open cup whose form is made up of two fishes (the early Christian emblem derived from the Greek word for 'fish', which gives the initial letters for 'Jesus Christ, Son of God, Saviour'). In the Cup is the paten for the Bread of the Communion. From a new tree, flanked by the signs Alpha and Omega, stems the Evangel as four angels holding Gospels from which arrows shoot in all directions. They stand in buildings, suggesting the Church in the four corners of the world, and grow into a final realisation of God, in the form of eyes open to all Truth.

(4) This window tells of Man's individual response to God's intervention. Many different shapes suggest, in analogy, many different individual reactions to God's initiative.

First, at the base, is the flower of manhood, shown by two shapes, themselves male and female, but containing form figures of budding ideas and conceptions.

Responsible life proceeds through a complex and hazardous circle with images of the good and the bad on either side. This with the arrow passing through horizontally symbolises the young man or woman confronted by physical and spiritual dangers.

The flame-like shape arising from the stem may represent passion, war or any human conflict symbolised in the analogy of the burning fiery furnace of the Book of Daniel. Salvation from the effect of this conflict is shown in the taller figure with the nimbus ('. . . one like unto the Son of God') who transcends the fire and turns its confusion into an ordinary flame.

There follows a passage of marriage and a quiet domestic life. This may be taken also as a mystical marriage of physical, mental and spiritual forces, from which alone true concepts are born, so that within the smaller compass of man's soul there is a kind of Incarnation (the triangular figure holding a cross).

From this state there grows a critical period when faith is tested in a world of contrary forces. The 'crux dissimulata' or distorted cross symbolises this.

From this new flux mature creation appears: in the physical world this is typified by the plan of the Cathedral spreading horizontally in time while from it growths of unified ideals stretch up vertically into a timeless flowering.

Conflict and Struggle–the third pair, numbers 5 and 6, multi-coloured

(5) Here is the struggle with evil powers for Man's salvation. The great Dragon of the Apocalypse is cast out of Heaven, pouring out floods, and dragging down the stars as he falls. The answer to David's cry of despair (the up-stretched hands) is shown in the great vision of the woman 'clothed with the Sun' surrounded by the praise of God through all kinds of instruments.

This window contains the assured faith that evil will eventually be overcome and cast out, and a pure, childlike faith will emerge tiumphant. This ultimate triumph of good over evil in the life of Man raises the design, as the window progresses upward, to a hymn of praise to God for Man's salvation.

(6) This window speaks beautifully of the struggle with evil in the world–the struggle with materialism, the struggle with indifference, the struggle with worldliness.

Maturity–the fourth pair, numbers 7 and 8, Blue and Purple

(7) The maturity of a life lived in faith in God blossoms as a flower in full bloom, coloured in the colours of peace and stillness. This is the reward not merely of those who are called saints, but of all Christians who have been faithful and whose hope is set in the Resurrection to life eternal.

(8) This window speaks of the maturity of suffering borne by Jesus Christ at the end of His earthly life. The Chalice – traced through the whole length of the design – contains in it all the accumulated sin and suffering of God's creation, which Jesus Christ lifted with Himself to the Cross in His Act of Redemption and Atonement, and prayed 'Father forgive' in relation to 'the sins of the whole world'. Here in this design is the depth of meaning of His prayer on the eve of His Crucifixion when He prayed in the Garden of Gethsemane 'Remove this cup from me: nevertheless not my will, but thine be done'.

The Chalice symbolises, too, the highest achievement of Man's skill and art – something worthy to be offered to God, as at the Holy Communion a chalice containing the wine of the Sacrament is lifted to God, or something which brings pain and agony to God as in Gethsemane. Here is an accurate analogy of the achievement of Man's genius either to relieve suffering and bring relief and joy to Man's heart or, on the other hand, to add to Man's fear and sorrow and bring grief to the heart of God.

A window depicting Eternal Reality

Eternal Reality – the fifth pair, numbers 9 and 10, Golden

(9) Man's search for a knowledge of the truth about God reveals this truth imperfectly to his understanding – as 'through a glass darkly'. Its main outlines are suggested by man's interpretation of his experience of God – God as the Creator, God as the Redeemer, God as the Comforter. And because Man's understanding of God – Three Persons in one God – is imperfect, the Godhead is presented in this window in abstract forms. (Incidentally, while each of the three artists created three windows, this window was the united work of all three.)

The colour of this window catches up the colour predominant in the 'flower of old age' window, and suggests that Man's journey to the 'Vision of God' when 'we shall see Him as He is' goes on after bodily death, the ultimate end of the journey of life being symbolised by the golden glory at the top of the window.

(10) As opposed to Man's uncertain understanding of the future life, the Resurrection of Jesus Christ was a passage to the absolute and glorious certainty of the Kingdom of Heaven.

Here in this beautiful golden window is the assurance of the

Detail of nave window

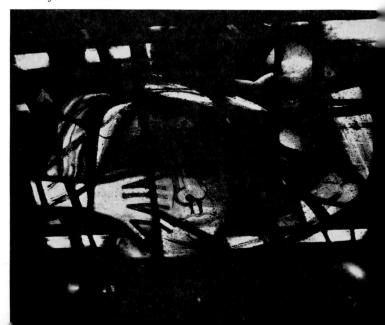

Heavenly City, the new Jerusalem, whose maker and builder is God. The scriptural basis of this design is Revelation Chapter 21 verses 9 to 26. An Angel measures the City with a reed, and speaks to the Evangelist. The kings of the earth bring their riches into the City and, above, the light of God shines into it.

The organ is placed on platforms on either side of the High Altar at the end of the aisles. The console is at the eastern end of the south choir stalls. The pipes of the organ are not obscured by an organ casing, though wooden louvres are used to improve the frontal design by obscuring some of the mechanical parts of the instrument. The organ was made by Messrs. Harrison and Harrison of Durham, and is an instrument of moderate size containing seventy-three speaking stops, four manuals and pedals. The instrument combines the best of the baroque and of the romantic periods.

The visitor now passes into the area of entrance to the Lady Chapel. Here, on the left, are the Swedish windows, also designed by Mr Einar Forseth, and given by the people of Sweden. The design of the windows represents the historic link between the Church of Sweden and the Church in England. In acknowledgment of this link with Sweden the steps which fall away from this landing down to the undercroft are referred to as the Swedish Steps.

The Lady Chapel is, of course, dominated by the great tapestry, 79 feet high and 38 feet wide. It is the design of Mr Graham Sutherland and it was made by Messrs Pinton Frères of Felletin in France. The central figure of Christ enthroned in glory looking in compassion on the world is surrounded by the four classical symbols of the Book of Ezekiel and the Book of the Revelation, interpreted by some to mean the four evangelists, by others to represent the four main categories of created power. In the middle, on the right, is a small portrayal of St Michael defeating the Devil. The lower portion of the tapestry, the Crucifixion scene, forms a reredos for the Lady Chapel, and on either side are representations of heavenly bodies.

In the Lady Chapel the visitor stands behind the High Altar Cross and cannot see it to its best advantage. This cross has a main design which suggests the Charred Cross in the ruins, with its irregular proportions, and set at its heart, as if held in

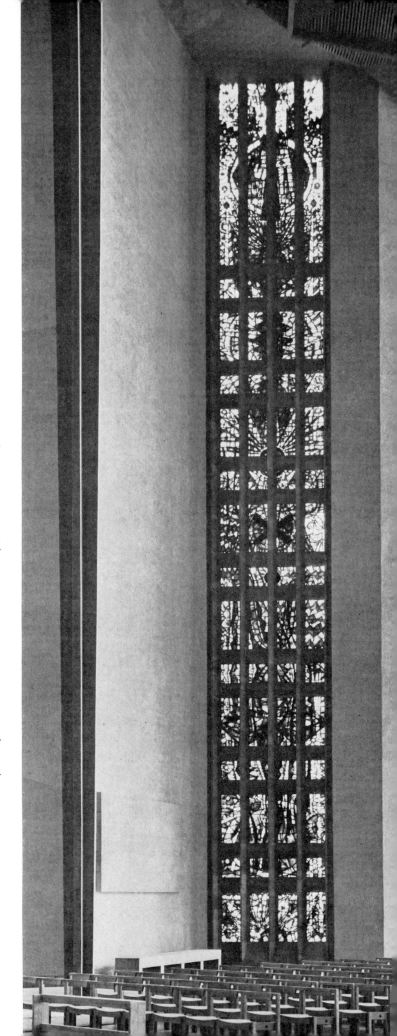

the palm of the hand, is the actual Cross of Nails which for twenty years stood on the High Altar of the ruins and is now replaced by another. The High Altar is of great simplicity, made of concrete with the surface hammered to make it rough like granite. An altar of concrete forming the heart of Christian worship in Coventry Cathedral makes an immediate link of association with the concrete city about it, which in its liturgy it tries to offer to God. The High Altar Cross was designed and made by Geoffrey Clarke.

From the Lady Chapel is clearly to be seen the mark and inscription of the consecration of the Cathedral on 25th May, 1962, by the Bishop of Coventry, the Right Reverend C. K. N. Bardsley.

Right: the Tapestry designed by Graham Sutherland, and below a detail showing the head of Christ

The High Altar Cross in silver and gold designed by Geoffrey Clarke

Right: details of Baptistry Window, designed by John Piper, made by Patrick Reyntiens

Far right: Baptistry Window from above

Nave windows reflected on the floor

Tapestry and Choir Stalls

Chapel of Unity and Porch
from the pedestrian way

View from behind altar of the old Cathedral

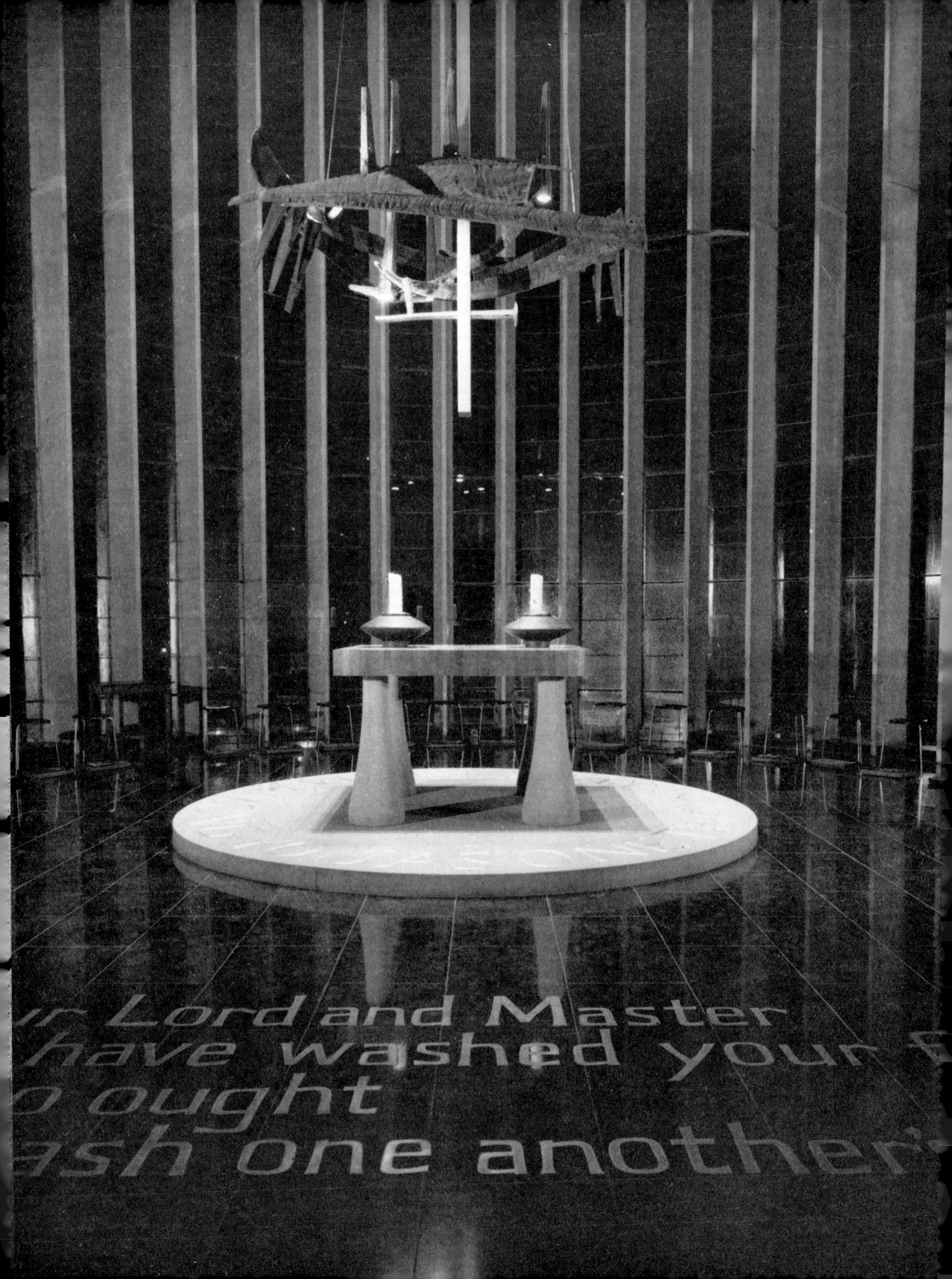
ur Lord and Master
have washed your
ought
ash one another

*Altar and floor in the Chapel of
Christ the Servant*

of all, a great rough boulder taken from the hillside of
Bethlehem and brought to the Cathedral in 1960 as the gift of
the Jordan Government, the Syrian contractor who packed it,
the Lebanese transport system and the Prince Line who conveyed it to Britain. Its final arrival, brought by Messrs John
Laing, the builders of the Cathedral, on Christmas Eve 1960,
surrounded it with particular significance.

Before leaving the Cathedral the visitor will wish to reflect on
some of the engineering features of it. Under the direction of
the outstanding constructional engineer, Mr Ove Arup, the
actual roof of the Cathedral is unsupported by any pillars. The
slender pillars coming down to a brass pin two and a half inches
square hold the free-standing canopy. Mr Ove Arup's feat in
creating this complicated engineering work is of outstanding
merit. Beyond the canopy are the lights of the nave shining
through a double row of ports. Also hidden behind the canopy
in the window recesses are the easily-operated television lights,
which can be lowered as required when the whole Cathedral is
converted to become a studio for the broadcasting of religious
services.

Printed across the great entrance to the Cathedral are the
words which summarise the whole concept of the interpretation of the history of the new Cathedral in relation to the old.
Out of the wrath of man can come the compassion and the love
of God. Out of Crucifixion can come Resurrection. Out of
Despair, Hope. This is summarised in this great text: 'To
the glory of God this Cathedral burnt'.

Out in the porch the visitor will have opportunities for quiet

Door knob designed by Sir Jacob Epstein

Baptistry Window and
St Michael's Steps with the old Cathedral
in the background

Detail of St Michael Overcoming the Devil

External view Chapel of Christ the Servant

reflection on what has been seen, for on the west side of the Queen's Steps are two chapels, both parts of the old Cathedral, the Wyley Chapel and the Chapel of the Cross. The Chapel of the Cross is a continuation of the name given to the transitional place of worship during the four years before the Cathedral was consecrated. It occupied the long space in the undercroft of the Cathedral and it was there, during the years preceding the consecration of the new Cathedral, that the congregation and the choir were built up. The cross designed and made by Geoffrey Clarke for the old Chapel of the Cross now finds its place in the chapel leading from the porch. The cross was originally designed to be seen from a distance and not at close quarters, and this fact should be borne in mind when it is seen in its final setting. Here in this chapel are some of the gifts given from time to time. The Jerusalem stone presented by the Governor of Jordanese Jerusalem; the Icon sent by the Patriarch of Moscow from Stalingrad Cathedral; another Icon which originated in Georgia in the Caucasus; a reproduction of the Our Lady of Vladimir Icon presented by a large group of Roman Catholics in the city of Coventry.

The porch leads down St Michael's Steps, so called because they are dominated at this ceremonial entrance to the Cathedral by the great bronze group of St Michael Overcoming the Devil. This is the work of the late Sir Jacob Epstein. Outside the Cathedral one is aware of the area of the undercroft. This houses the BBC sound broadcasting studio and television control room, the choir practice rooms, a lecture hall, the library (the joint gift of the City of Kiel and a Bedworth merchant, Mr A. E. Dewis) and the Navy Room, which serves as the social meeting room for distinguished visitors to the Cathedral and at all times for the clergy of the diocese of Coventry. The Chapter House, the Provost's Room, the clergy staff rooms, stores and the assembly area complete the provision of this great undercroft.

At this level is also the Cathedral Refectory, an acknowledgment of the need that those who worship together should have opportunities of meeting more personally. The Cathedral Refectory has become not only a place of refreshment for some of the hundreds of thousands who visit the Cathedral during the year, but also a place where the Cathedral staff can continually meet one another and meet the visitors.

The Youth Hostel, named John F. Kennedy House, completes the present provision of the Cathedral's facilities and forty young people may occupy it at any time. During the summer it is continuously occupied by groups of students from many nations who live, work and study in the Cathedral for periods of a fortnight or more. During the rest of the year it is used continuously at weekends by youth groups and student groups from all over Britain.

The intention of all these provisions is an attempt to project an image of a creative Christian centre for the whole community, a place of meeting, a place of unity, and within the context of divisions a place of reconciliation.

Exterior of the Chapel of Unity

The Coventry Cathedral Ministry

Cathedrals have been great at many periods in English history. At many points when the nation has required leadership the Cathedrals have grown to great stature as places of learning, artistic development and social advance. After the end of the Dark Ages leadership was provided by the great Christian work of Alfred at Winchester, followed immediately by the equally great work of Dunstan at Glastonbury. If the vast throbbing life of contemporary England needs a central principle of cohesion, interdependence and unity, and if these qualities are in any way the gift of the Christian faith, then the Cathedrals of England have a very great responsibility to establish themselves as creative community centres, articulating the needs of the community in a way which local parish churches can never hope to do.

To achieve this, Cathedrals obviously must justify their existence on far wider grounds than their musical tradition, or their great architectural beauty, or their rich history, or the holding of occasional diocesan services. Equally, for Cathedrals to match the opportunities and the needs of the present day they will need far more viable constitutions which will give them the flexibility and resilience to adapt their techniques and policies to the rapidly changing situation in the community about them. Changing a Cathedral Constitution is as slow and as cautious as changing anything in the kingdom, and even the recent revision of the Cathedral Constitutions in 1963 has not succeeded in equipping the Cathedrals with the flexibility necessary to face their task as creative community centres.

Broadly speaking, there are two types of constitution in English Cathedrals: those governed by a dean and chapter of a varying number of residentiary canons, and those governed by a provost, with a Cathedral council holding the corporate legislative authority, and a chapter of honorary canons being the trustees for the properties of the Cathedral and an advisory body to the bishop and the provost in Cathedral matters. Generally, the latter Cathedrals are those which are of more recent establishment, and were originally parish churches. Some, in fact, are still the effective parish churches of considerable parishes.

In 'dean and chapter' Cathedrals, the dean is the president of the administrative chapter, each of whom has authority within the corporate body of the chapter. It is clear that 'authority' becomes more of an issue, and not less, in such a situation, and equally clear that proposals for any new venture must first overcome the hazard of disagreement in the chapter. In many chapters canons whose individual service spans a generation–a generation, moreover, of the very changes in the community which are making urgent new demands on the Church–tend to regard change with suspicion or hostility. In the absence of a constitution which provides 'one captain for the ship' progress can be, to say the least, very slow, and fraught with much frustration.

In 'provost and chapter' Cathedrals, the situation is not uniform. In some there is in practice a greater degree of corporate authority than was intended in their constitutions. In some the authority of the diocesan bishop within the Cathedral is stronger than in others. In general, the parish church Cathedrals are likely to gain by the constitutional revision authorised by the Cathedrals Measure of 1963.

Coventry Cathedral is one of the newer Cathedrals, though the Cathedral consecrated in May 1962 is the third to be built on the present site. The first was built in the eleventh century and was, jointly with Lichfield Cathedral, the seat of the bishopric of Coventry and Lichfield. In 1538, St Mary's Priory in Coventry was destroyed, and Coventry was not again the seat of the bishop until 1918.

Coventry is one of the most ancient industrial centres of Britain. It was noted for the excellence of its craftsmanship in the thirteenth century. Its most continuous characteristic has been its adaptability. No industrial development has failed to be reflected in its skills and crafts over the centuries. It was the natural centre for the motor industry when this was begun. Its great factories were readily adapted to the manufacturing needs of the First World War, and its 1914 population of 90,000 doubled during the four years of the war.

It was, therefore, as the centre of a vigorous modern industrial area that the fourteenth-century parish church of St Michael was chosen to be the Cathedral of the new diocese of Coventry in 1918. Industry continued to expand, so that when the Second World War started in 1939 a heavy concentration of factories making armaments, aeroplanes, cars and many precision instruments made Coventry an area likely to be attacked from the air. On 14th November, 1940, accompanied

by an emotional atmosphere of great bitterness, the centre of Coventry was subjected to the first mass attack endured by any city in Britain in that war. As the war continued, the scale of this attack was seen to be very small compared with the hideous destruction by fire and explosive of many other cities in Britain and Europe. But Coventry was the first, and its name reached every corner of the earth.

St Michael's Cathedral died in flames with the city around it on 14th November, 1940. From the moment of its destruction, true to the rhythm of Crucifixion followed by Resurrection –the heart of the Christian religion–it was resolved to rebuild it. But the resolve was to do more than to restore a building. The old Cathedral was destroyed in hate and Christians may not leave open wounds of hate unhealed. Human hope had by that act been crucified on a world stage and it was on a world stage that the drama of forgiveness, reconciliation and resurrection had to be enacted. Every act of hate, bitterness and destruction leaves humanity at a parting of two ways: either to entomb hate and bitterness and to erect memorials so that they will not be forgotten, or to 'roll away the stones' from these tombs and let hope rise again. The first of these choices makes it certain that the circumstances of hate and bitterness will be repeated. The latter makes it certain that the vision of hope will be made brighter, and the power of hate diminished by a little.

This was the chosen path of Coventry Cathedral, and it has set out to demonstrate in the context of its own history and its own community the central Christian truth of Reconciliation, which is capable of continuous demonstration in every Cathedral which has a relationship with the diverse, and often divided, community around it.

Coventry Cathedral was fortunate in its establishment in a city whose administrative and industrial leaders are far-sighted and vigorous. The civic authorities no less than the leaders of industry had already given thought to a new city before the

The modern pilgrims to the Cathedral

war gave them the compulsion to build it. But in laying their plans for a new city, the civic authorities have studied community trends, transport and communication probabilities and population implications for housing and education, and have tried to anticipate them.

Here is an analogy of the great need of the Church – to study precisely these massive trends and probabilities, and to try, by its strategic planning, to anticipate them.

In general, cities which for centuries contained a coherent and integrated community, living and working within it, have become metropolitan centres densely surrounded by an expanding suburbia.

Within the centre is the organisation and administration and the control of public services upon which suburbia, and much beyond it, depends. As has been said, relationships at that level are largely impersonal. Where the community becomes personal, in suburbia, the tendency is to localise the population areas in such a way as to induce both isolation from the metropolitan centre, and from each other. 'Housing Estates' and ecclesiastical parishes are not conducive to consciousness of belonging to a total community embracing industry, commerce, administration and social responsibility, as well as to the more intimate community of the immediate locality, and we do not create a community merely by calling it a local community.

It is for reconciliation within the larger community that Cathedrals should equip their ministry; and because the new city of Coventry contains in a definable area all the main characteristics of our changing society – industrial, social, commercial, housing, rapid population growth – a definable situation has been presented to the Church which the new Cathedral is trying, in its varied experiments, to grasp.

index

Italic figures indicate pictures

COM
ALLYE
AND I
MY YOK
FOR I AM
AND YE SI